# Book Of Shawdows

## 150 Spells, Charms, Potions and Enchantments for Wiccans

ISBN: 978-1986816175
The rights of Shadow Books, to be identified as the Creator of this Work have been asserted in accordance with the Copyrights, Designs & Patents Act 1988.

# Introduction

This book contains 150 Magickal spells from all over the globe and space for you to write and create your own.

Casting a spell comes in virtually an unlimited number of forms. Some spells have words spoken; others may be thoughts. Some use potions; others use candles; others again may involve botanicals.

There are many ways to cast a spell, and all are as equally effective based on one core component: Belief.

Your belief in the power of magick. Your belief in what you are doing – that it can, and will work. It is about what your goals are, and what your intent is.

Also, it is important that you pick spells that feel uniquely right for you. This will heighten their effectiveness. If you are not drawn to chanting or working with botanicals then find a spell that works for you.

With over 150 spells to choose from, these have been split into the many different areas of life. Trust your intuition and learn from the contents of this book. Refine and remould based on what feels right to you.

If you have fear, worry or concern when casting a spell. It won't work. If you are focused on what you don't want – that is what you will create for yourself.

When you cast any of these spells or the spells you create yourself the key is that you need to be in a centred, open-hearted, open-minded space. And that you view the very thing you are wishing for as yours now. You focus on having it versus wanting it. As that is what will be brought back to you – what you believe you have already is what you will indeed have. What you want – you will continue to want.

# Contents

# Harmony

## Spell for Peace & Harmony

Items Needed:

- ❧ Rose Quartz
- ❧ A Mirror
- ❧ A Pink Candle

Light the candle & place it in front of the mirror. Hold the rose quartz in your hands and gaze at the flame reflected in the mirror as you chant the following:

> O blessed & reflected light
> Bring to me peace this night
> Let my mind & heart be free
> And filled with love & harmony

Look past the flame into the mirror. Try to see which negative elements are affecting you that you want to get rid of. See them being drawn from you into the candle flame and then into the mirror.

When you feel the time is right, place the mirror face down. Allow the candle to burn for one hour and then snuff it out. Clean the mirror in salt water and repeat whenever needed.

## Jewels Of Wisdom

❦ To lift your spirits, light a green candle and hold jade whilst meditating

❦ Carrying a quartz crystal will create tranquillity around you

❦ If you are feeling overwhelmed of under duress, hold a black obsidian.
If the stress is caused by an overabundant workload, keep the obsidian in
or on your desk.

## Candle Calm

You can create a week of blissful and composed calm with the following spell.
On a waning-moon MONDAY evening, anoint a black or grey candle with
violet essential oil. Please the candle on your altar beside a vase of fresh
violets or other purple flowers. Sit in front of your Altar as twilight begins,
and when the sun is completely gone, light the candle and chant:

Care and woe, beggone
I am the mountain, the river, the tree, the grass, the moon
I receive my strength from Nature and she is my center
Tomorrow and the next, all gladness will enter

# The Serenity Spectrum

For a Peaceful Home
Burn blue candles on Thursday

To Overcome Fear
Burn red candles on Sunday

For Inner Peace
Burn silver candles on Monday

For Self-Confidence
Burn red candles on Sunday

For Physical Wellbeing
Burn green candles on Friday

To Overcome Regret or Guilt

Burn white candles on Wednesday
For Mental Clarity
Burn yellow candles on Wednesday

To Let Go Of Anger
Burn orange candles on Monday

For Success at Work
Burn green candles on Friday

# Conjuring By Colours

Harm to none, only good. Colour Magick is a basic tenet for working spells. The properties of each colour determine how it impacts your mood, frame of mind, and the potency of your spell casting.

Be mindful of the colour of the candle, gemstone, and flower you choose; carefully pick the hues of your clothing, furniture, and even the paint on the walls.

For example, if you are given to moodiness or anger, remove all RED from your home décor. If you are predisposed to melancholia, a VIOLET scheme may depress you.

# Happy Home Spells

## Peaceful Homes Spell

*Items Needed:*

- ❧ One Blue Candle
- ❧ Tranquillity Oil (equal amounts of ylang ylang, rose and lavender oils)
- ❧ Sandalwood incense

This spell is especially useful for those who entertain on a business level. There are times when people of varying viewpoints may need to come together in a social atmosphere. To keep things running smoothly, harmoniously, and peacefully use this spell before the party.

One hour before the party take a ritual bath. As you are doing this, begin to visualize the guests as they arrive, seeing in your mind's eye the evening progressing and everyone having a wonderful time.

When you finish bathing, anoint your solar plexus with the tranquillity oil. This will help you project a positive and harmonious energy level throughout the evening.

Take the blue candle and place it in the room where most of the evening's activities will be held. Now light the incense and carry it throughout the house, saying, as you move from room to room:

Queen of heaven, star of sea
Fill this house with love and harmony
Silver goddess enthroned above
Let all gather here in peace and love

Just before the guests arrive, enter the room where you have placed the blue candle and light it. Walk in clockwise around the room four times, chanting just as you did in the other rooms. Place the incense next to the candle and wait for your guests.

## Alum Spell

Alum magically 'eats' negativity.

- Place Alum in dishes
- Discreetly arrange to eliminate negative feelings and behavior
- Replace at least once a week  *Do not consume the alum yourself and keep out of reach from children & animals. *

## Vanilla Spell

- Stick a vanilla bean into a tightly sealed canister of sugar.
- The aroma will infuse the sugar: use it in your cooking and feed it to your family, to instil feelings of peace, contentment and happiness.

# Vervain Happy Home Spell

Vervain is considered the friendliest botanical. Unlike other botanicals, which are said to display an ambivalence towards people, vervain is believed to love us and crave our presence and delight in bestowing us with good fortune.

Surround the home with it. Vervain's magickal protection is desirable, plus you'll always have a fresh supply.

Create infusions by boiling water over vervain and sprinkle this liquid throughout the house to maintain happiness and good cheer.

# Joy & Laughter Oil Spell

Add essential oils of sweet orange, lime and pink grapefruit to a base of jojoba oil. Dress candles with this oil and burn throughout the home to instil joy & laughter.

Spread the joy! By soaking cotton balls with Joy & Laughter oil and carry them in your pockets, so that the joy travels with you.

# Happy Home Oil

Add gardenia petals, myrrh and a pinch of five-finger grass to blended jojoba and coconut oil, together with a pinch of salt.

Place droplets around the house, or dress candles with the oil.

# Blue Bird of Happiness Spell

Rare blue flowers confer peace and protection on a home. Grow cornflowers, delphinium, bluebells and hydrangeas. Reserve the blossoms; dry, grind and powder them, and then sprinkle the powder discreetly through the home.

# Death in The Family Spell

In the event of the death of the 'head of the family', the main protector or income provider; preserve a lock of his or her hair. Nail it beside the lintel of the main entrance with an iron nail to maintain the household's prosperity and protection.

## Basil Happiness Spell

Surround your dwelling with fresh basil so as to draw and increase joy within the home, and to stimulate tranquillity, harmony, cooperation & peace.

- Grow basil in your garden
- Place pots of fresh basil by your front entrance and around the perimeter of your home
- If it's not possible to grow basil, then place fresh basil in a vase in a prominent spot in your kitchen, replacing it weekly or as soon as it starts to spoil.
- Cook with it as much as possible, or incorporate it into spell work (basil also draws love and money towards you)

## Family Unity Spell – To Heal Rifts

To heal rifts and to maintain the unity of the family, you will need one hair from the head of each person in the family or each person involved in the rift, whatever you deem appropriate.

- Braid them and tie together with a red silk thread
- Wrap the braid in more red silk thread, winding it and making seven knots in it.
- Wrap this in a small square of white silk
- Bury this packet at a crossroads.

# Home Protection Spell

* Collect rocks and pebbles from your travels, especially from places where you felt safe and happy.
* Charge them in your hands and hold them to your heart
* Keep them in open terracotta pots
* Use to cast circles for ritual or protection as needed.

# Negativity Begone

Cast this spell on a happy day that has an ambience that you would like to preserve forever. Blend cumin with sea salt and scatter a circle around the perimeter of your property to banish negativity and dissension whilst focusing on happy thoughts.

# Oil On Troubled Water Spell

* Pour Olive Oil on the exact spot where an argument or unhappy confrontation or scene of humiliation occurred.
* Let it stay for a little, to absorb the tension and negative energy, before cleaning it up.

# Protection Spells

Protection spells provide magickal protection and are to be used in conjunction with taking common sense approaches to protecting yourself from any harm. Be that having locks on your doors, or seeking professional help if you think your safety is being threatened.

Protection spells will protect you most from malicious spells, hexes or negative enchantments cast deliberately against you by another. As well as protecting you from an assortment of spiritual dangers than may have been caused deliberately or inadvertently.

The number 5 along with the numbers 7 and 9 are all magickal numbers most associated with magickal protection.

Colours red, black and blue are the colours most associated with magickal protection.

## The Witch's Protection Bottle

Items needed:

One small jar, and enough of the following items to fill the jar:

- Broken Glass
- Nails
- Thorns
- Steel Wool

- Wormwood
- Thistle
- Nettles
- Vinegar
- Salt
- Your own urine
- One Black Candle
- One red felt market

Fill the jar with the items listed above and seal tightly. On the top of the lid, draw a pentacle with the red felt market. Place the black candle on the lid of the jar and light it. Chant the following over the candle:

Candle of black and hexes old
Release the powers that you hold
Reverse the flow of spells once cast
Leave pain and sorrow in the past

Let the candle burn out. Take the jar and bury it in the earth close to your home. It will protect you and your family from harm. In most cases it will form a shield of protection for about six months. When the spell begins to weaken, make a new protection bottle.

# Aloe Vera Protection Spell

Aloe vera's leaves, filled with healing, soothing gel, are shaped like spears. Maintain living plants on your altar for spiritual protections, especially if working with volatile entities or dangerous spirits (which we do not recommend that you do!).

# Aura of Protection Spell

Arrange blue crystal gemstones strategically around your home or the area you wish to protect. This creates a magickal boundary to keep out evil.

# Hex Breaking Spell

Obtain the bark of the Wahoo Plant (do not ingest this for any reason) from your herbalist. This plant is known as 'Euonymus atropurpureus'.

Steep the bark in boiling water. After it has cooled, dip your right index finger into the liquid and cross your forehead saying seven times loudly 'Wahoo!'

Other commonplace herbs that ward of unsettling energy are:

## Lemon Rind
Rubbed on furniture, doorjambs, and window frames, cleanses negative energy

## Rosemary

When added to potpourri, woven into a wreath, or sprinkled on your doorstep, helps protect you

## Salt

On the threshold of your home will keep away unwanted guests

## Botanical Guardian Spell

These nine herbs provide protection against all manner of evil. Feature them in a garden to surround you with spiritual and magickal protection.

- Chamomile
- Chervil
- Crab-apple
- Fennel
- Mugwort
- Nettles
- Plantain
- Watercress
- Flax

## Box of Chocolate Spell

Chocolate possesses the power of transform enmity into friendship. Make a peace offering with a box of fine chocolates. This will only work however if the other party will eat REAL dark and bittersweet chocolate.

# Vetiver Protection Spell

Vetiver's strong scent lingers protectively. This spell is performed when bathing.

- Create an infusion by pouring boiling water over dried vetiver roots.
- Allow this to cool, and then add the strained liquid to your bath.
- Alternatively, add several drops of the essential oil to a tub filled with comfortably warm water.

# Salt Scrub Protective Shield

Salt scrubs are applied directly to your body. Using a gentles or vigorous circular motion. The oil causes the other ingredients to cling to the body even after rinsing. This is an extremely powerful way to create a cleansing and protective shield.

- One cup of salt to one cup of oil
- Store in an airtight container – it will last indefinitely based on water not getting into the container
- Castor oil is the most protective carrier oil and should be added to the scrub, however it's extremely thick and doesn't always blend well. Add other carrier oils and play with proportions until it pleases you.

# Iron Protection Spells

Iron provides protection 24 hours a day, whether you are asleep or awake.

- Bend a used horseshoe nail into a ring
- An iron bracelet reinforces the magickal protective capacities of the hand
- String iron beads and wear around your neck and ankles
- For protection while you sleep, slip a knife or a horseshoe under your pillow
- Or a sword or fireplace poker under the bed
- Or sleeping in a bed crafted from iron creates an island of safety, reinvigorating health, creativity and fertility while you sleep.

# Red Brick Dust Doorstep Spell

Red brick dust protects against malevolent magick and repels evils of all kinds.

- Smash an old red brick with a hammer until sufficient dust is obtained
- Add red brick dust to a bucket of floor wash and scrub the front steps and threshold area
- Sprinkle powdered red brick dust over the threshold daily before sunrise.

# Healing Spells

Healing spells are not intended to be used in place of traditional or conventional (allopathic) methods of healing. They work best in conjunction with them as a reinforcement, enhancing the power and likelihood of healing.

Tradition asserts that the full moon is the best time to initiate healing spells because as the moon diminishes, so should the pain and illness.

In general with healing spells often someone else must cast the spell on behalf of the ailing person (this is different to most other categories of spells). However most spells do require the presence and sometimes the participation of the ailing person.

## Peppermint Distance Healing Spell

- ❧ Place Peppermint leaves on top of a photograph of the patient
- ❧ Charge a blue candle with your desire
- ❧ Carve and dress the candle as desired
- ❧ Burn it beside the photograph
- ❧ When the candle has burned down, dispose of the peppermint leaves
- ❧ Repeat as needed, with fresh leaves each time.

## Rosemary Infusion Of Power

Washing your hands with an infusion of rosemary magickally empowers and enhances all healing.

Create an infusion by pouring boiling water over rosemary. Allow it to cool, then strain. This may be done immediately prior to healing or the liquid can be bottled and refrigerated for use later.

## Bear Journey Dream Spell

A dream bear is seen as a powerful visualization technique when you know what ails you but you don't know how to treat it. Bears are repositories of traditional medical wisdom.

- Take the image of the bear to bed with you. Three-dimensional images are best, and it needs to be more 'bear like' than cute. The beauty of a 3D bear is that you can hold it in your hands whilst you journey. Alternatively if all you have is a photo image or similar – work with what you have.
- Prepare yourself for sleep – have all lights off. And begin your dream while you're awake.
- Visualize your bear – the dream bear does not have to look like your image/3D bear.
- Visualize the scenario where you meet the bear, hop on the bear and tell the bear what you need to find a remedy for. Then let the bear take over.

- At some point you will most probably fall asleep, although some people achieve waking visualizations. The journey should continue in your dreams. Repeat this exercise as needed until the information you require is received.
- Make sure that at the end of the visualization the bear returns you to where you began. If this doesn't happen in your dream, work with it while awake.

## Color Therapy

Every color has the capacity to heal. Each color has specific magickal powers best suited for certain ailment or physical conditions.

Expose yourself to concentrated doses of the color(s) most powerful in their healing properties for your ailment. Surround yourself with this color, wear it, gaze and meditate upon it.

- Black: physical and mental exhaustion
- Blue: emotional imbalance, post traumatic stress, throat disorders, speech disorders, headaches, toothaches, insomnia
- Brown: vertigo, disorientation
- Green: physical healing, cancer, ulcers, high blood pressure, heart trouble
- Orange: bowel and digestive disorders, arthritis, asthma, fevers, bronchitis and related bronchial ailments
- Red: physical disabilities, blood disorders, HIV & AIDS, anaemia, vitamin deficiency, impotence, infertility

🐝 **Yellow**: stomach problems, skin disorders, depression due to heartache

You can also access this healing magic of color through:

🐝 **Crystals** – although crystals have their own specific healing powers, generalities may be made due to color. Select crystals in the color most beneficial to you and use them in massage, meditation, and other healing rituals

🐝 **Color baths** – tint the water so it co-ordinates with your healing needs.

🐝 **Candle Magick** – select candles in colors that correspond to healing your ailment.

## Earth-absorbing Healing Spell

Chant the following nine times with the desired result that you affliction is magickally transported from your body and absorbed into the Earth.

I think of you

Hell my _____ (fill in the blank)

Let Earth retain the illness

Let health remain with me.

Put your hands flat on the Earth and spit.

# Stinging Nettles Spell

Keep fresh stinging nettles under the patient's bed. Replace them daily, burning the old nettles.

# White Sage Healing Spell

*lavendar sage*
Dont use white sage!!!

~~White sage~~ is considered one of the most potent cleansing and protective botanicals. For maximum benefit grow your own to use.

Burn quantities of ~~white~~ sage to magickally drive away illness

# Knot Healing Spell

This involves tying and untying the string.

- ❧ Tie seven knots in a string
- ❧ Visualize the illness and suffering as you tied the initial knots (you are not wishing the illness – in fact the opposite. You are transferring the illness into the knot)
- ❧ Make it into a bracelet for the patient
- ❧ Untie one knot each day – visualizing the relief as the knots are untied, as the illnesses negative energy is allowed to dissipate into the atmosphere.
- ❧ On the last day, unravel the thread and throw everything into running live water, flowing away from the patient's location.

# Spell For Healing Burns

- Gather 9 bramble leaves
- Place them in spring water
- Murmur over each leaf:

> Three ladies came from the east
> One with fire, two with frost
> Get out with you fire!
> Come in with you frost!

Pass the leaves over the afflicted area (you do not need to touch the wound, as the energy of the leaves near them will reach the burn area)

# Get Rid Of A Common Cold Spell

Minimize and ward off chills by wearing a tightly beaded amber necklace. Amber is seen to absorb body heat and retain it, thus magickally creating a balancing effect.

# Amazonite Healing Spell for Sore, Weak Eyes

Place an amazonite crystal gemstone in pure spring water overnight. Use the water to bath sore, weak eyes.

# Ovarian Shield Spells

According to metaphysical wisdom ovarian disorders are linked to intense criticism, whether from others or self-criticism. Every sharp criticism is an arrow aimed straight at the ovaries. It is about erecting a physical shield.

- Dilute one drop of rose attar into sweet almond oil and massage it over the ovarian region, for protection and to promote self-love and acceptance.
- Make a magick girdle by stringing charms, amulets and cowrie shells on red cord.
- Place red quarts crystals over the area. Visualize a shield that lingers after the crystals are removed.

## Hematite Headache Charm

Place a Hematite crystal gemstone over the spot where your head throbs. Amazonite and jet may be used in a similar fashion!

# Luck & Success Spells

## Blessings Of Good Fortune Spell

To bless something or someone, scatter elder leaves and berries to the winds, circling sunwise murmuring the name of the person or thing. Scatter some more directly onto the person or thing if possible.

## Metal Key Spell & Wind Charm

Metal keys attract positive magick into your life and at the same time deflect evil.
Magick keys open doors of opportunity. The best keys to use are old metal keys – which can be found at flea markets or antique stores.

- String together a collection of old keys onto a red thread as a charm or wind chime.
- Hang the keys in the wind to rustle up beneficial opportunities.

## Bread Spell

- Nail a slice of bread behind the front door
- Fasten purple ribbon to the nail
- Replace as soon as the bread begins to rot or deteriorate, burning the old slice.

# Stop Opposition Incense

To overcome opposition to your success, burn the following botanicals as incense:

- Cloves
- Garlic
- High John the Conqueror
- Jezebel Root
- Licorice
- Sweet flag (calamus)
- Woodruff

Grind and powder the botanicals, sprinkling onto lit charcoal or burn the bruised botanicals in a cauldron.

Burn the incense in the room where opposition is most likely to occur.

# Vervain Spell

The sacred herb vervain is believed to turn bad luck into wonderful luck, attract love & prosperity and make even your enemies like you.

- Make an infusion by pouring boiling water over vervain
- Once the infusion has cooled, bring it to the tub (don't strain the botanicals out)
- Undress, get into the water and pour the infusion directly over you, then soak in the bath.
- Allow yourself to air dry.

# Lucky Clover Bath

Make an infusion by pouring boiling water over red clover. Let it cool, strain and add it to a tub filled with warm water so that you're bathing in clover.

# Lucky Charm Bracelet Spell

Choose a charm that represents your goal. At the new moon place this charm beside a small pink candle. Charge the candle with your desire, carve and dress it if you life and burn the candle

When the candle burns out, attach the charm to a bracelet. Wear it or reserve in a safe place – whatever feels right for you.

When this goal is achieved set another goal, choose another charm and begin again.

# Ginger Root Spell

Ginger root is believed to bring joy, fun and happiness into your life.

Macerate ginger in sunflower and jojoba oil until you've achieved the desired intensity of fragrance. If you have fresh ginger plants add the blossoms to the oil too (you may also add a few drops of essential ginger oil for added intensity – this has been known to be a skin irritant so take care with it).
Strain the ingredients and reserve the scented oil. Apply this oil behind your knees, elbows and ears when striking out for adventure.

## Break Bad Luck Spell

Carve your affirmation and desires on a white candle and dress it with olive oil.

Roll it in ground red pepper.

Light the candle, place it securely on the floor and jump over it.

## Happy Time Powder

Blend the following ingredients together:

- Dried ground strawberry leaves
- Dried powdered vanilla bean
- Finely grated orange zest

Sprinkle this powder around the perimeter of your home, behind doors and in all its corners, for a change of luck and improvement in your fortune.

## Out With Bad Luck: In With The Best Luck Spell

Burn the candle at both ends – eliminate misfortune and because nature abhors
a vacuum, simultaneously attract something positive to replace it.

- Obtain one red & black double action candle. It may be necessary to trim the bottom of the candle so as to expose the wick so that both ends can be burned simultaneously.

- Carve what you wish to eliminate from your life on the black end.
- Carve what you'd like to see manifest in your life on the red end.
- Ideally, place the candle horizontally on a candlestick holder with a spike. Alternatively drive a long nail through the line where the colors begin and end, thus dividing the colors.
- Place the candle horizontally over an open bottle, inserting the nail to balance it out.
- Burn both ends simultaneously!

## Full Moon Lunar Wish Spell

Stand naked in the light of the full moon. Bath yourself in the moonbeams as if you were bathing yourself in water.

Gaze at the moon whilst doing this, when ready make your wish.

Watch for an immediate response: if the moon remains clear, it's a positive sign.
If the moon brightens and the light intensifies this is an even more auspicious sign.

If a cloud passes over the moon you can anticipate some difficulty in achieving your desire. Take further magickal steps or perhaps reassess your desire.
Work on it until the next full moon and repeat.

# Love & Romance Spells

Tips for Successful Romantic Magick

## Timing:

Friday coinciding with a New Moon is considered the most auspicious time to perform love spells.

Friday's in general are the best days for love spells.

The day is names in honor of Freya, Northern Lady of Love. It is also the day associated with other powerful spirits of love – Aphrodite and Oshun.

## Colors for Love Magick:

Yellow
Orange
Pink
Red

## Numbers:

Two: the standard number – for the obvious reason
Five: if you'd like to invoke the power of Oshun, Orisha of Love
Six: if you'd like to invoke the power of Aphrodite, Lady of Love
Eight: if you'd like to invoke the power of Inanna-Ishtar, Queen of Heaven.
Eight: is also the number of infinity and eternity.

Bathe your hands in rose water prior to mixing up any love potions or powders to intensify their effects.

If you find that your love spells are consistently not working place a strand of your target's hair under a continuously dripping faucet to magickally wear away resistance (remember too that we are to always allow others to have free will, and wish for what is the best for us and the other person when we cast our spells).

## Amber Charm – Dreams Of Desire

On a Thursday night make a list of the qualities you desire in a romantic partner or visualize and name a specific person. Before you go to sleep that night, leave a piece of amber by your bed or under your pillow.

On Friday morning, first thing upon awakening, clutch the amber in your left hand, holding it close to your heart.

Close your eyes and visualize your desire. Make it as real and tangible as possible – as if you are with them now – you HAVE what you desire. Take as much time as you need.

Kiss the amber and wrap it up in a small piece of silk, wrapping or rolling towards you.

Keep this with you for seven days, carrying it by day, sleeping with it as night, beside your heart, between your breasts, wherever.

Repeat the process every morning. At the conclusion you will have a highly charged love-drawing amulet.

# Bring The Love You Want To You Spell

Find a photo or draw a picture that represents the person who you desire to be with (or reconnect). You may or may not be in this photo as well.

Create a sacred space or altar that includes items that feel energetically positive to you (for love you may want to include rose quartz crystals and/or figurines that show loving couples).

Hold this picture in both hands and meditate with it, and see yourself and this other person as if you are already together. If it is marriage you desire - feel into the feelings you would have if you were married already.

Feel the joy you would feel of being together. Meditate on this for about 5-10 minutes.

Then place the photo in your sacred space. And as you go about your life, when you think of this person and yourself, always think of being in the relationship you desire to have with them as if you had it now.

Clear out any doubts or fears that it is anything other than that.

By having this constant positive focus, energetically and magickally you will draw that person to you.

Do not worry, wonder, or plot the 'how', simply keep your focus on you being with them together as a couple, happy and in love as if that was your reality right now in this moment.

(Remember no one has to know what you are thinking, so do not allow yourself to buy into others projections or judgements on what is real, possible or appropriate).

## Arrow Spell - Eight of Wands

One of the traditional meanings of the eight of wands tarot card is love at first sight. The eight wands represents the arrows of love.

- Carve and dress a red candle as desired, using love-drawing oils.
- Burn the candle
- Place an eight wands card upright near the candle so it is easily visible.
- Once the candle burns down, place the card underneath your pillow so that it can provide romantic insight and inspiration while you sleep.
- During the day wear rose quartz in a charm bag, pocket or tucked into your bra to attract and maintain the love you desire.

## Lodestone Love Spell

Lodestone's magnetic properties are used to draw love towards you and then keep that love close at hand.

Lodestones are believed to have genders, just like other living creatures. Their gender is determined by their appearance: the rounder looking ones are female, while the males are the more phallic looking stones.

Choose lodestones to match your desires, use one to represent yourself and another to represent the person you would like to draw into a romance.

- Choose a lodestone that represents you and soak it in 'Come to Me Lover Oil'
- Sprinkle it with magnetic sand and place it on the edge of a mirror
- Choose a lodestone that represents the person you wish to draw into romance.
- Soak this one in 'Amor Oil'
- Sprinkle with Magnetic Sand and place it on the mirror, on the opposite edge of the first lodestone.
- Carve a candle dedicated to romance and dress it with 'Lucky Lodestone Oil'
- Light it and focus on your wish for romance and move the two lodestones slightly closer to each other.
- Pinch out the candle
- Repeat this daily until the lodestones meet in the middle, and then allow the candle to burn all the way down.

## Come To Me Lover Oil

Jasmine absolute
Rose attar
Neroli or essential oil of petitgrain
Gardenia absolute (or fragrance oil)
Tuberose absolute

Blend the above into apricot kernel or sweet almond oil.

This is the most deluxe love-drawing oil. The ingredients are extremely expensive. It is not required that all of them be used, although the first three are fairly standard. The substitution of petitgrain for neroli will keep the costs down.

## Amor Oil

Place a balm of Gilean bud and a piece of coral inside a bottle
Cover these with sweet almond and jojoba oils
Add a few drops of either petitgrain or neroli essential oil plus a drop of tangerine essential oil Add a bit of ground cinnamon or one drop of essential oil of the cinnamon leaf.

## Lucky Lodestone Oil

Add crushed, powdered lodestone to Van Van Oil.

## Love Attraction Spell

Items needed:
- One pink candle
- A small dish
- A heart-shaped locket
- Basil
- Rosemary
- Thyme
- One thing green velvet ribbon
- Rose Oil

The spell should be performed on a Friday night as close to the full moon as possible. Place all items called for on a small table that will serve as an altar. Take time to visualize the one you wish to attract. If you have a photograph of the individual you wish to attract, place it on the table as well.

Take the candle and inscribe your name on one side and the name of the person you wish to attract on the other side. Connect the two names with intertwining hearts, then anoint the candle with the rose oil as you chant the following seven times:

[Insert name] your thoughts are of me
No other face shall you see

Set the candle on the dish. Fill the locket with some basil, rosemary and thyme.
Hold the locket close to your heart and say the chant seven more times. The placing the locket next to the candle, light is as you chant the following:

With herbs and flame I hold thee tight.
I make thee mine from this night.

When the candle has completely burned out, hang the locket from the green ribbon and give it to the one you desire.

# Red Witch Candle Spell

Candles in the shape of red witches are particularly beneficial for love magick. The imagery is always positive as the red witch may represent the power of witches as an ally or she can represent female power. The red witch is also symbolic for the menstrual blood that figures in so many love spells.
Red Witch candles are used to draw love.

This spell may be used for an unknown lover of for someone who you already desire. If you know the person's identity, insert their name into the chant.

- Anoint her with love drawing oils
- Chant the following:

### Red Witch, Red Witch
### Bring me my lover

- Light the candle for a set period of time nightly. Choose a number that has significance for you – six minutes, nine, an hour. What is crucial is that this period of time be maintained consistently.
- Burn nightly until burned down.

# Candle Love Spell

Items needed:

- A picture of the one you desire
- Some of his or her hair
- Some of his or her handwriting

- A red cloth pouch
- A red image candle (of a person of the same sex as you)
- Rose petals
- Rose oil

On the night of the new moon, gather all of the items needed and place them on your altar. Pick up the image candle and hold it lovingly. Focus on the candle and visualize the one you desire. When you feel the time is ready anoint the candle with the rose oil as you chant.

Candle of power
From this hour
Bring unto me
The love that I see
That he/she shall requite
My love from this night
Let him/her only see me
As I now will, So Mote It Be

Allow the candle to burn completely out, fill the pouch with the rose petals, the phot, the handwriting, and the hair. Anoint the pouch with the rose oil as you repeat the chant. Whenever you plan to be with this person, be sure to have the pouch with you. Once the relationship is on solid ground, hang the pouch over the entrance to your bedroom for lasting love and happiness.

# Make Her Love You Spell

Fumigate your clothing with the scent of aloes wood, cinnamon, and myrrh to attract women's romantic attention.

AND

Hand a woman a sprig of basil. The belief is that is she accepts, she'll fall in love with you and remain faithful forever.

## Grapefruit Spell To Lure Another Woman Away From Another

Cut a grapefruit in half.
Write the woman's name and her present lover's name on a piece of brown paper.
Write your own name over the lover's name, so that the original lover's name is now illegible.
Stick this paper into the center of the grapefruit.
Put inside a disposable pan or baking dish or line a permanent pan with foil.
Sprinkle the grapefruit with salt, pepper, and brown sugar.
Arrange five golden candles around the grapefruit and light them.

# Follow Me Boy Spell
## (for women wanting to attract men)

He may be forced to follow you but he'll be happy to do it!

Dried sweet flag (calamus)
Dried catnip
Dried damiana
Optional: add licorice if you like the fragrance.
Also add essential oils of bergamot, sweet orange, tuberose plus essences of any red flowers.

- Powder the dried ingredients together
- Add them to sweet almond oil, shaking to blend
- Finally add any essential oils

To use dip a cotton ball in the oil and tuck it into a bra or pocket.

Or wear the oil as a perfume. This is reputed to be very powerful and will draw men to you like flies, so be selective when approached.

# Shoe Spell

To turn a sexual relationship with a man into something more:

- Pick up his shoes as soon as he takes them off.
- Place your own shoes inside his, you left inside his left, your right inside his right.
- Buckle or tie them together as securely as possible
- Leave them like this until morning

# Right Person Love Spell

You don't want just any lover, you need the right one!

This spell is wonderful for those looking for a long-term love.

Add Attraction Oil to your bath every Friday until you have found the love you want.

## Attraction Oil

Grated lemon zest
Lovage
Vervain
Essential oil of lemon petitgrain, Melissa, may chang or lemon verbena
Rose attar

- Grind the first three ingredients together in a mortar and pestle
- Place them in a bottle together with a lodestone chip
- Cover with sweet almond oil
- Add the essential oils, drop by drop, until you achieve a scent that pleases you.

## Seeking New Love Spell

Soak Catnip in good whiskey overnight, ideally in the light of the full moon. Strain it out and sprinkle the liquid on your doorstep for 21 days in the shape of a new crescent moon.

## Seeking A Certain Someone Special Spell

This is a spell to persuade someone to return your affections.
You need three candles: two figure candles – one to represent you, the other to represent the person you desire; the third is a large pillar or heart shaped candle.

* Arrange the two figure candles six inches apart
* Place the third at the apex of the triangle
* Dress the candles, ask for what you want to have happen (remember to phrase it as if you have it now i.e.: [name] and I are happily married), and light the candles.

## Self Love Spell

Before you can receive love from another you must love yourself. Roses, hibiscus and calendula stimulate and teach self-love, self-forgiveness and self acceptance.

* Add fresh blossoms to your bath
* Make infusions from dried flowers and add to your bath
* Surround yourself with bouquets and loving plants

## Talisman Of Love – Red Ribbon Spell

To discover a bit of red ribbon, string, wool or piece of fabric indicates luck in love and a change in romantic fortunes. Pick it up and make a wish. Carry the ribbon as an amulet.

## Talisman Of Love – Rose Quartz

Rose quartz is believed to draw lovers towards you. Wear it as jewelry or carry it with you.

## Apple Romantic Cleansing Spell

A cleansing spell for when a bad love affair has resulted in you feeling unloved, tainted, humiliated or defiled.

* Dice an apple and douse the pieces with honey and cayenne pepper
* Let it sit until it rots
* Flush the pieces down the toilet
* Affirm that you will learn to love again but more wisely this time.

## Broken Heart Bath

❧ Add white rose petals, honey suckle blossoms and rose attar to a bath filled with water.

❧ Place a rose quartz large enough to not go down the drain in the bath too

❧ Soak in the scented bath

❧ Following the bath, carry the rose quartz with you. Sleep with it under your pillow until you don't need it anymore.

## Lover Come Back Spell

This spell is believed to return a departed lover within twenty-one days. It possesses a protective aspect as well as a summoning one. If the spell doesn't work and he's not back in the prescribed time, this may mean you are better off without him. Start making new plans.

❧ Create an infusion by pouring boiling water over damiana and red rose petals.

❧ Bathe in it. When you're done, reserve some used bathwater in a bottle.

❧ Add a little of your own urine and sprinkle some of this liquid in front and back of your home for twenty-one days.

# Marriage And Divorce Spells

## Getting Engaged Spell

- Use a conjoined bride & groom candle or two figure candles side by side.
- Carve and dress the candle(s)
- Bind them with ribbons, knotting in desires and blessings
- Perform a marriage ceremony over the candles, using your name and that of your beloved.
- When you have pronounced them husband and wife, burn the candle

## Happy Marriage Duck Spell

Ducks are believed to mate for life. A pair of mandarin ducks serves as a lucky charm in the hopes you will be able to emulate the devotion to each other. These ducks epitomize faithfulness and fidelity.

Post a pair of mandarin ducks prominently in your home. Or place a matched pair of statues somewhere strategic to radiate happiness there.

## Happy Marriage Tree Spell

Surround your home with magnolia and pine trees to provide a shield to preserve and protect your happy marriage.

# Forsake the Other Woman Spell

This spell is designed to make the husband/ partner forsake the 'other woman'.

- Go to a crossroads barefoot with your head uncovered and your hair loose and undone.
- At the crossroads pick up a pebble and place it under your left armpit
- Make a wish: along the lines of 'as I remove this pebble from the road, so to the other woman is removed from my husband/ partner's heart'
- Go to a second crossroads
- Pick up another pebble but this time place it under your right armpit. Make the wish again.
- With both pebbles in place, go to a third crossroads and pick up another pebble.
- Stick this pebble between your breasts or beneath your chin and repeat your wish.
- Go home: when you reach your residence just outside drop all the pebbles into the gutter.

## In Law Spell

Oregano is believed to keep meddlesome in-laws away. Greek oregano is believed to be the most powerful variety of the species.

Rather than cooking with the oregano for your spouse's troublesome parents, sprinkle it around the premises instead. You may also want to sprinkle it on their photos as well.

# Be True Charm Bag

- Place caraway, cumin, and coriander seeds in a red charm bag
- Add pine needles and an unadorned gold ring
- Ideally this should be sewn into your partner's clothing, but it may be placed underneath the mattress on his side of the bed too.

# Divorce Candle Spell

This is a spell for the person who would like a divorce while the other party is resistant.

- Obtain male and female figure candles
- Place them back to back, ready to go in opposite directions
- Dress them with 'Command and Compel' Oil and burned in timed increments, corresponding to the number of years you have been wed.
- If you were wed for 20 years burn them for 20 minutes. Pinch them out when the time is up.
- Next day before lighting the candles again, move them further apart.
- When they are finally as far apart as space will allow, let the candle burn entirely
- Each day as you perform this ritual – visualize you two apart – as if you have achieved that result already.

## Command and Compel Oil

Sweet flag (calamus) blended with Licorice and reduced to a powder
Vetiver (optional) Essential Oil of bergamot (optional) Add to a blend of castor oil and jojoba oil.

## Lavender Safety Spell

Lavender is believed to minimize spousal abuse and cruelty

a) bathe in a bath with lavender essential oil added to it
b) safety pin a sprig of lavender inside your clothing

# Fertility Spells

Fertility spells are not limited to people wishing to have children. They may also be used to enhance and stimulate artistic creativity as well. Adapt these spells to best suits your needs.

## Astarte Oil Candle Spell

Astarte Oil is believed to promote personal fertility. It includes:

- Essential oil of coriander
- Essential oil of jasmine
- Essential oil of myrrh
- Essential oil of petitgrain or neroli
- Rose attar

Blend all ingredients along with sweet almond and jojoba oils and place into a bottle. You can also add cowries, henna twigs and blossoms to the oil.

This oil is to be used for dressing candles and charms – and is not to be used on your skin whilst desiring for pregnancy or during it.

- Obtain a human figure candle that represents you
- Carve it with your name, birthday and identifying information, affirmations and desires.

* Dress the candle with Astarte Oil, particularly the abdominal and genital areas of the candle
* An additional step is to roll the candle in henna powder
* Burn the candle

## Basil Spell

Basil is believed to encourage fertility.    Plant basil around the home or maintain abundant potted plants.  Place basil plants in window boxes or beside the door to signal your wish for fertility to earth's spiritual forces.

Hang fragrant bundles of basil over the bed to enhance successful conception. Keep the basil fresh, green and aromatic – replacing when needed.

Add basil to your diet – pesto, in salads.

## Cowrie Shell Spell

The sea is seen as a font of fertility and any seashell radiates and transmits that power.  The most powerful of seashells is believed to be the Cowrie.

Cowrie belts worn over the reproductive area are an ancient and believe to be potent magickal solution to encourage fertility.

* String Cowrie shells into a belt long enough to wear over your hips
* Make sure it falls over your ovaries and inner reproductive organs.
* Tie your intentions into each knot.
* Wear your belt whenever and however you like, for maximum effectiveness wear your belt under the Full Moon.

# Egg Candle Spell

Eggs are one of the oldest and most powerful fertility symbols.

This spell has you creating your own strong powerful egg:

- First make the candle mould: gently punch a small hole in the large end of a raw egg
- Use a cuticle scissor to cut a small circle of eggshell (you may need to practice with a few eggs before you get skilled at this)
- Empty the egg contents into a bowl
- Gently wash the inside of the shell with water. The membrane and all contents must be thoroughly removed. Allow it to dry completely.
- Prepare the wax (you can also add tiny fertility charms or herbs)
- Use the egg carton as a holder. Place the eggshell, hole end up, in the carton
- Pour in the liquid wax, reserving a little (when its half full you can add tiny seed beads, charms or herbs – however the candle is effective without them)
- Let the wax harden overnight
- Next day gently heat the reserved wax until liquid again.
- Gently chip away the shell, exposing your candle.
- Heat an ice pick or similar thin sharp tool. Put through the center of the candle and gently thread with a wick.
- Fill the hole with the hot wax
- Decorate – keep as an amulet or burn in a spell.

## Fertility Tree Spell

❧ Choose an existing tree or transplant a grown specimen

❧ Nurture the tree. Develop a relationship with the tree.

❧ Embellish and decorate this tree

❧ Charge fertility amulets, charms, and spell ingredients by hanging them on the tree or placing them at its base overnight, especially in the light of the Full Moon

❧ Offer libations to the tree

❧ Sleep under the tree

❧ If possible make love under the tree.

## Contraceptive Knot Spell

❧ Make knots in a cord for contraception, knotting in your desires, goals and intentions

❧ Reserve the cord in a safe and private place

❧ Place the cord in a glass of water

❧ Let it soak overnight, then drink water

❧ When you're ready to conceive, untie the knots

# Pregnancy & Childbirth Spells

## Anti-Miscarriage Spell

A knot spell can assist with setting a safe due date.

At first sign of miscarriage, make a tight knot in a strong cord.
Visualize the knot as your baby.
Talk to it:
As this knot holds firm, so you hold firm in my womb.  Do not loosen until
[ insert due date or select a date]
Place the cord in a secure covered container or wrap it up in a baby blanket
Keep it in a safe place.  Be sure to untie the cord at the appropriate time

## Miscarriage Prevention Spell

Collect amber, coral and cowries – any size will do.
Cast a circle from amber, coral or the cowries and lie within it, either on the
floor or on the bed.  Place amber, coral and/ or cowries against your pregnant
belly and maintain calm.  Breathe deeply into your chest and your stomach
and let go, and trust that you and your baby will be fine and all will be well.

## Birth Chamber Aroma Spell

Warm essential oils of clary sage, jasmine, and lavender in an aroma burner to welcome the baby, soothe the mother and relax all involved.

## Eased Labor Spell

Prepare this charm/ amulet prior to delivery.   Create a necklace of coral beads with a lodestone suspended from it, and wear during the delivery.

## Infant Protection Spell

Hang bunches of chamomile over the baby's crib for magickal protection.

# Youth, Beauty & Longevity

## Aphrodite's Beauty Spell

Goats are considered sacred creatures. Soak violets in goat's milk and wash your face with this for beauty.

## Egg Beauty Spell

Eggs are perceived as magickal and powerful. Reserve the water used to boil eggs. Let it cool and bathe with it for youth, vigor, and beauty.

## Lunar Beauty Bath

The planet of magic, romance and feminine power the moon offers the gift of beauty.

- Stand naked in the light of the Full Moon
- Go through the motions of bathing in the moonbeams and absorb their beauty
- Ask the moon to help you with whatever troubles you – whether it be weight loss, hair growth or any perceived imperfections
- Now watch for an immediate response from the moon. If there is no change – that is considered a positive response. If the moon brightens that is extremely encouraging. A sudden darkening or clouding suggests that you can expect some challenges to your request.
- If the latter reconsider your request
- Repeat as needed at each Full Moon.

# Anti Baldness Onion Spell

Cut an onion in half and rub that half vigorously over your exposed scalp, twice daily, morning & evening.

Or if you have too much hair for the above to work, instead juice an onion and blend with a shot of vodka and a tablespoon of honey.   Massage this mixture into your scalp, leave for 30 minutes, then rinse out of your hair.

# Hair Growth Spell

Blend the essential oils of clary sage and ylang ylang together, and rub into your scalp every night to promote hair growth.

# Weight Adjustment Spell

Not unlike what Elizabeth Taylor is reputed to have done on the door of her refrigerator, draw an outline of a human figure that corresponds to your present reality (or use an existing photo).

If you would like to lose weight, draw a second figure inside the first demonstrating what your preferred shape should look like.

If you would like to gain weight, draw a second figure around the first, to show what it is you would like your silhouette to resemble.

Post the image where you can see it as encouragement and burn candles of your choice beside it for reinforcement.

Please know that weight loss or gain does not happen overnight, and you also need to support with a healthy diet and exercise campaign.

## Weight Loss Gem Spell

Moonstone or topaz are thought to regulate metabolism. Where either of these gems to encourage weight loss, or to stabilize your weight, as desired.

## Beauty Longevity Spell

Like fine wines, certain fragrances grow more beautiful with age. Anoint orrisroot with a drop of ylang ylang and/ or patchouli oil and carry with you in a red silk bag so that you too will only grow more fine and beautiful with age.

## Honeysuckle Longevity Spell

Surround yourself with living honeysuckle to encourage longevity

## Anise Renewed Youth Spell

If you feel like your life experiences have aged you, and/ or you are feeling older than you would like to feel, a magickal remedy is to hang fresh sprigs of anise from your bed. These are believed to restore your youthful nature.

# Prosperity

**Primary Number:** 2 – because it encapsulates the concept of doubling

**Primary Colors:** green and gold

**Planets:** Jupiter – because it is the planet of good fortune; the Moon, because it's the planet of magick and fulfilled wishes; and Mercury because the Roman God whose name it bears is involved with prosperity and finance.

**Lunar Cycle:** Spells for any form of financial growth, debt recovery, increase in money or business, is recommended to be done with the waxing moon.

## Money Drawing Candle Spell

*Items needed:*
- One green candle and holder
- Lavender Oil
- A pen or sharp pointed object

For best results begin this spell on the first night of the waxing moon. Gather the items called for and place on a small table to serve as an altar. Relax and visualize the amount of money you need. Pick up the candle and inscribe your name near the top of it.

In the middle draw a large dollar sign. At the bottom of the candle write out the exact amount of money you need.

Next anoint the candle with the lavender oil. Be sure to rub the entire candle with the oil. As you anoint the candle chant the following:

Money, money come to me
As I will, so it shall be

Place the candle in the holder and light it. Gaze into the flame of the candle and repeat the chant.

Allow the candle to burn for four hours and then extinguish it. Repeat the spell each night until the full moon. On the night of the full moon allow the candle to burn out. You should receive your money before the next new moon.

## Basil Bath Spell

The scent of basil on the skin allegedly attracts financial good fortune to the wearer. Take this bath before engaging in any interaction revolving around your finances.

- Roughly chop most of a large bunch or basil, in order to release the volatile oils, but leave some leaves whole, especially those that remind you of cash bills.
- Pour boiling water over the basil and let it steep
- When it's cooled, add this to your bath. Float the whole leaves in the water and visualize yourself swimming in cash,

* Let the water drain and allow yourself to air dry
* Do not dispose of the used basil leaves (don't throw out the cash!) but either leave them in the tub until your transactions are complete or remove them, place in a bag and reserve until an opportune moment for disposal arises.

## Magic Bean Spell

There was more to 'Jack & The Beanstalk' than you may realise. Sometimes fairy tales do come true – and beans are actually thought to be a tremendous source of wealth in the magickal world.

Collect 3 yellow or gold beans, murmur your desires over them and charge them with your energy of your commitment to your goals.

Carry the beans with you in a charm bag along with a lodestone.

## Magic Coin Spell

String three coins together. Place them on or under your telephone to stimulate prosperous business.

## Basil & Bergamot Money Spell

* Write the exact sum that you require on a square piece of brown paper
* Carve your name, identifying information and the sum onto a green candle

- Dress the candle with essential oils of basil and bergamot
- Place the candle over the paper
- Burn the candle for increments of 15 minutes daily until the specified amount has accumulated.

## Money Growth Candle Spell

- Carve and dress a green candle to express your financial desires
- Place it on a suitable plate – round is better
- Arrange coins at the base of the candle
- Light the candle and chant:

Money grow, money flow
Candle burn, watch me earn
Money grow, money flow
Flame shine
What I want is mine

- Repeat this three times whilst visualizing you have the money you want and how that would feel.

# The Wallet Spell

First up withdraw or change notes/coins for a $100 bill and put it into your wallet or purse. Keep it with you at all times, and whenever you hold your wallet or purse, remember that your $100 bill is there.

Feel pleased that it is there, and remind yourself often of the added sense of security that it brings to you.

Now as you move through your day, take note of the many things that you could purchase with $100. Remind yourself each time that you see something that you like, that you could purchase it because you have $100 in your wallet.

By holding the $100 and not spending it right away, you receive a vibrational advantage each time you even think about it. So if you were to remember the $100 and spend it on the first thing you noticed, you would have received the benefit of feeling your financial well being only once.

Now if you mentally spent that $100 bill 20-30 times in that day, you have received a vibrational advantage of having spent two or three thousand dollars!

Each time you acknowledge you have the power, right there in your wallet, to purchase this or to do that, over and over again you add to your sense of financial wellbeing so your point of attraction shifts.

And as you feel more abundant you will magickally attract more abundance.

# Ginger Root Spell

Sprinkle dried powdered ginger in your pocket or purse to increase your finances.

AND

Bury whole ginger roots in Earth to draw money towards you. For added intensification, arrange in auspicious patterns such as a diamond or pentacle.

## Wealth Incense:

Combine brown sugar, ground cinnamon and ground coffee.

Add powdered (confectioner's) sugar, carnation petals, garlic chives and cherry blossoms (or apple blossoms or blossoms from any flowering fruit tree – leave out if you can not find them).

Grind all of the ingredients together.

Burn outside your front door of your home or business to attract wealth.

Leave the ashes alone for 24 hours to radiate their power, then dispose of them in nature or in living running water (stream, river....).

# Grow Some Cash Spell

This spell is designed to stimulate your finances to grow.

Plant coins in a pot filled with dirt (crossroads dirt is the most potent). Plant a basil plant in the pot. Make sure you tend to this plant regularly. Touch its leaves gently daily so that its money enhancing energy is infused into your being.

# Vervain Spell

A sprig of vervain kept in your wallet or purse acts to keep money there.

# Seven-Eleven Money Spell

- Carve your desires into a black or green cat candle
- Dress it with money drawing oil, and sprinkle with gold, green, red and/or purple glitter
- If you need a specific amount of cash, write your request on a slip of paper and place it under the cat.
- Light the candle for 7 minutes the first night, 11 the second, 7 the third, and so on, alternating between the lucky numbers 7 and 11 until the amount is received.
- If the candle burns down completely without receipt of the funds, this too is an answer: the whole situation needs to be reconsidered as well as new alternatives.

# Knot In Your Hair Spell

Comb or brush your hair.

Visualize the money you need. As long as you are visualizing allow yourself to visualize big.

When nine strands of hair have been caught in your come or brush stop brushing. Start chanting:

I need [amount]
Please bring me [amount]
Be specific

As you're chanting, rub the strands of hair between your palms, forming a string. When you've created a long chord of hair, tie nine knots in it, moving from left to right.

Visualize the money in your hand as you hold the hair. Visualize your debts paid. When you are ready either bury the hair in the Earth or burn it.

# Loan Spell

Blend essential oils of bay laurel, frankincense, myrrh and sandalwood into a base of sweet almond and jojoba oils.

Massage this combined oil into the soles of your feet before bedtime and also before applying for a loan.

# Collecting Debt Spell

Place a photograph of the person who owes you money on a plate. Use a piece of paper with the person's name on it if you do not have a photo.

Sprinkle with powdered sweet flag, licorice and bay berry.

Light a green candle on top of the powdered photograph and burn it.

See your debtor paying you back with ease and good grace while the candle burns.

# Career & Business Success

## Basil Better Business Spell

- Shred approximately one half cup of fresh basil leaves.
- Cover the basil with about half a litre/ a pint of boiling water.
- Let the basil steep in this water for 3 days.
- On the fourth day strain out the water, reserving the liquid.

Sprinkle this liquid over the entrances and thresholds of your business, in corners, behind doors and near any places where money transactions occur. You want to have this in any spot that may be considered vulnerable.

The belief is that it attracts customers and prevents theft.

## Dream Job Spell

- Get a fresh piece of green paper
- Write on this what your dream job is – be very specific. What you would be doing, what you would be paid, who you would be working for, where you would be working – again be very specific
- Anoint it with a few drops of basil essential oil
- Carry it around with you and focus on visualizing as if you have your dream job already.

## Job Interview Success Spell

Sprinkle sea salt into the palm of your hand. With the palm in a cupping position raise your hand closer to your face and share your desires relating to this job you are going for.

Place a portion of the salt in your pockets prior to the interview. Place some salt in your brief case or any other bag you may be taking to the interview.

If possible sprinkle a small amount of salt over the threshold of the office or in the office close to the interviewer's desk or chair – do so without taking unnecessary risks – as carrying it on your person alone will enhance your chances.

## Basil & Honey Spell

* Chop fresh basil into fine threads
* Warm honey gently over the stove
* Add the basil to the honey and simmer
* Remove the basil-honey mix from the heat
* Chant this spell over it:

Flies flock to honey

Customers flock to me
Bears flock to honey
Business flocks to me
Ants flock to honey
Contracts flock to me
(this can be adapted to your specific situation)

- Run a warm bath
- Rub the honey over your body before entering the bath
- Soak in the water for a while. Then as draining the water when finished, reserve some of the used bathwater.
- Toss this water on the grounds of your business.

## Magic Coin Better Business Spell

- String 3 coins together or purchase them already linked
- Place these strung together coins on top of a yellow or golden cloth
- Sprinkle magnetic sand over the coins
- Anoint with bergamot essential oil
- Roll and fold the cloth toward you so it forms a packet
- Tie securely with red silk ribbon
- Place this packet inside or near your cash register, phone, computer – wherever you do business – for increased business and wealth.

## Job Interview Self Confidence Bath

This bath is magickal in that it is designed to increase self-confidence and personal magnetism so your chances of success are increased.

Take the bath just prior to the interview or the night before.

- Place allspice berries, cinnamon sticks, cloves, whole nutmegs and pieces of sandalwood in a bowl
- Cover with boiling water and let the botanicals steep for at least an hour

❧ Draw a bath for yourself while this is happening
❧ Stand in the tub and toss the now lukewarm infusion over your body
❧ Soak and steep yourself in the bath
❧ Allow yourself to air dry when finished

## Orange Candle Job Spell

Perform this spell in conjunction with the New Moon.

❧ Write a description of your dream job on the back of a copy of your resume.
❧ Brush the resume with honey and sprinkle it with magnetic sand.
❧ Fold the resume nine times
❧ Anoint an orange candle with Van Van Oil while you visualize your employment dreams coming true.
❧ Roll the candle in gold sparkles.
❧ Place it atop the folded resume and burn

Van Van Oil

A blend of five wild Asian grasses (can come as essential oils):
- lemongrass
- citronella
- palmarosa
- gingergrass
- vetiver

Added to jojoba, sunflower and/ or safflower oils

# Better Business Floor wash

Combine ground cinnamon, brown sugar and red brick dust.

Add this to a bucket of water, together with white vinegar.

Use this mixture to wash your floors so as to attract better business.

# Legal Spells

## Legal Victory Over Adversaries Spell

❧ Write the names of all adversaries or potential ones, on individual pieces of paper. Include the judge, attorneys, opponents and their witnesses etc.

❧ Place these individual pieces of paper on a dish

❧ Cover with honey, strawberry syrup and wine lumps or spoonfuls of white sugar.

❧ Carve a purple candle and dress it with Commanding Oil

❧ Place the candle on the dish and burn it

❧ When the candle has burned completely bury all of the remnants including the pieces of paper in the Earth.


Commanding Oil

Blend:
- sweet flag (calamus)
- licorice

Reduce to a powder and add:
- Vetiver
- Bergamot

Mix into a blend of castor and jojoba oils.

# Red Pepper Name Spell

This is a spell that is designed to encourage reconciliation and empathy among parties involved. Perform this spell 14 days before the court proceedings begin.

- Slice a red bell pepper in half and remove the seeds
- Write the names of all of the parties involved in your legal proceedings
- Put them inside the pepper and add dillweed and coriander seeds
- Fit the halves of the pepper back together, sealing it shut
- Place it in the freezer and keep it there until after the final legal resolution.

# Friendly Judge Oil

Two parts dried carnation petals
One part anise seed
One part ground cinnamon

- Blend the above ingredients together, grinding and powdering
- Place the powder inside a bottle
- Olive oil encourages justice, castor oil creates a protective effect, and jojoba oil brings victory (as well as being a natural preservative).
- Fill the bottle containing the botanicals with one of a combination of these carrier oils
- Add a hematite or bloodstone to the oil for extra benefit.

Carry soaked cotton wool balls with you and if possible rub the areas near the judge or where you are seated for best effects.

# Tongue Control Spell

This spell is designed to put a stop to gossip, slander and testimony against you. For the best results perform this spell at the center of a crossroad or standing at a window.

A sudden gust of wind is an extremely auspicious sign.

❧ Blend a pinch of white sugar, pinch of flour and a pinch of fine ground salt.

❧ Hold the powder in the palm of your hand whilst visualizing your desired outcome.

Chant:

I am innocent of all accusations
Protect me
( you can call on the spirit/ deity of your choice)

❧ Allow the powders to fly out of your hand


# All Purpose Justice Spell

Hold a brown candle in your hands. Close your eyes and focus on your current situation and then feel into and imagine it all being sorted now. You do not need to work out 'how' this will happen. Simply focus on feeling free of any injustice or pressures relating to your current situation.

When the candle feels charged, light it and allow it to burn.

# Weather Spells

## Drought Spell Sieve

Pour water on a parched ground through a sieve.

## Make It Rain Spell

Toss raw rice into the air to simulate rain.

## Rain Frog Charm

Create little images of frogs.  Place the frogs on hilltops or where there is raised ground and charge each with the mission of calling in the rain.

## Stop The Rain Spell

Draw and cut out a figure of a woman holding a broom in her hand.
If the rain becomes dangerously excessive, hang the figure under the eaves and pray for it to dry up.

Appeal to the figure for assistance.  The belief is that the figure will use her broom to sweep away the clouds and rain so the sun can shine through.

## Lightening Protection

Marjoram is believed to ward off lightening. Keep it around your home for protection.

## Heat Relief Spell

If threatened with dangerously intense heat, offer chamomile to the sun to honor and appease it. Request and pray to the sun to ease off its heat.

# Protect Against Theft, Regain Lost Objects

## Amethyst Theft Protection

Wearing an amethyst is believed to protect you against pickpockets and thieves.

## Vetiver Personal Protection Spell

Bath in water infused with Vetiver essential oil. This is believed to create a magickal aura of protection against harm.

## Licorice Theft Protection Spell

Use the licorice herb. Place a stick of the herb in each corner of your property like a stake. This is to protect from break-ins, theft and vandalism.

## Anti Theft Caraway Spell

Burn caraway seeds as incense in your home. This is thought to protect your home from theft.

## Horseshoe Spell

- ❧ Finding a horseshoe has long been known to be auspicious, this can also be a sign from the universe that you will find your missing article.
- ❧ Keep an eye out for unorthodox horseshoes as much as the 'real' kind. It could be a charm, jewelry or an image.
- ❧ Drive the horseshoe into your fireplace so its firmly fixed
- ❧ Visualize what was lost back in your hands.

## Regain Stolen Money Spell

Rub a drop of pine essential oil into your hands. Use another drop to dress a pinecone. Hold it over your head and twirl it around sunwise requesting that the stolen money be returned to you.

# Banishing Spells

Difference between a banishing spell and a binding spell:

- **Banishing Spell** – remove something or more frequently someone from your presence, often permanently
- **Binding Spell** – attaches something or more frequently someone to you with great intensity, often permanently

## Begone Banishing Powder

Grind the following ingredients together:
- Black peppers
- Cayenne Pepper
- Cinnamon
- Sea Salt
- Sulfur

Sprinkle the banishing powder on clothes, especially belonging to anyone you would like to see gone (without wishing harm to them)
This powder can also be used as an accompaniment for spells, particularly around or over candles.

## Change or Else!

This spell is designed to request that the target either reforms or leaves peacefully.

- ❧ Using castor and olive oils as a base, add patchouli and vetiver essential oils.
- ❧ Rub this on the door knobs of your target's home

## Banish Your Bad Habits Bath

Add the following essential oils to a bath filled with warm water:

- ❧ Clary Sage
- ❧ Frankincense
- ❧ Lavender
- ❧ Lemongrass
- ❧ Rosemary

Enter the bath and as inhaling the fragrance visualize clearly what habits you want to break. Focus on the images in your mind and accompanying feelings as if you already have mastered that habit and it no longer is an issue for you.

## Eating Disorder Banishing Spell

This spell should coincide with the waning moon.

❧ Using olive oil as a base add fennel essential oil

❧ Dress a small black candle with this oil

❧ Hold the unlit candle in your hands and visualize the pain and bad habits flow from your body into the candle.

❧ When you feel as if you have purged yourself of all negative urges and emotions in this moment, put the candle down and pick up a moonstone in your left hand, and clear quartz crystal in your right.

❧ Bury the candle not too close to your home. Place the crystals in a pretty charm bag and keep them with you all the time, cleansing them frequently, and re-charging as needed.

## Banishing Gossip Clove Spell

Sam Ropka?

Cloves are used to stifle and end gossip.

Grind cloves into a powder. Sprinkle the powder onto lit charcoals: fumigate your body, clothing and premises to halt malicious gossip about you.

# Rotten Apple Banishing Spell

- ❧ Cut an apple in half horizontally, so that the star in the center is exposed.
- ❧ Rub one half of the apple with a mint leaf whilst visualizing what needs to be banished
- ❧ Put the two halves of the apple back together again
- ❧ Stick with a skewer through the pieces, so that they will remain joined
- ❧ Tie the pieces securely together with black silk or stain ribbon
- ❧ Bury the apple. Your problem should dissipate as the apple rots.

# Antidotes to Hexes & Reversing Spells

### Antidote Red Brick Dust

Red Brick dust is a powerful magickal remedy (if you cannot access red brick dust you can use: ground hematite, henna powder or red ochre.

Smash an old red brick with a hammer to obtain the dust, add it to a bucket of water and cleanse wherever you know of suspect a hex was laid.

You can also spread the red brick dust around the perimeter of your home (or even inside if you feel that is necessary).

Sweep it out with a ritual broom.

Dispose of the broom after sweeping or reserve for similar use.

### Cayenne Hexbreaker

Sprinkle cayenne pepper throughout the home to break any malevolent spells.

### Chamomile Hexbreaker

Sprinkle chamomile around the perimeter of your home and property to break any spells against you.

## Reversal Candle

Obtain a new seven-day candle. Turn it upside down. Carve the bottom of the candle so that the wick is not exposed and may be lit.

Slice the top of the candle so that it can stand. Dress the candle. If you know the name of your jinxer, carve that into the candle.

Light the wick and chant:

Candle let the evil done against me reverse itself as I have reversed you

Say this nine times whilst visualising the weight of the curse being spirited away into nothing.

## Hydrangea Hex Reversal

Burn dried Hydrangea to reverse spells and remove hexes. Blend the ashes with more dried, ground hydrangea and scatter around the home.

And to close on a positive, loving note:

## Love Attraction Spell Extra Strength!

- Select, carve and dress a candle to represent the object of your desire.
- While the candle burns, write your own name on a piece of paper with invisible ink.
- Sprinkle the most fragrant flower petals available over the paper and fold towards the candle
- Hide this in your target's underwear drawer.

# Notes

# Obsession spell

write both full names on a slip of paper

fold it towards you tightly

spray the paper with your perfume

kiss the paper with your favorite lipstick

putt this paper in a small box or jar

optional: adding crystals, herbs etc;

leave in closet for ten days

after ten days remove the paper burn the paper with a white or pink candle.

bury the ashes in the front yard

Started 8/4/21

Made in the USA
Middletown, DE
26 July 2020